Usborne
Sticker Dolly Dressing
Fashion Long Ago

Designed and illustrated
by Stella Baggott

Written by Lucy Bowman and Louie Stowell

Historical fashion consultants:
Rosemary Harden and Anne Millard

Contents

2 Ancient Egypt
4 Ancient Rome
6 Ancient China
8 Medieval times (1200s)
10 Spain in the 1500s
12 France in the 1770s
14 England (1810)
16 Victorian times (1890s)
18 England in the 1920s
20 America in the 1950s
22 London in the 1960s
24 Design your own
   Stickers

Ancient Egypt

In a scorching sandy desert, a Pharaoh, his wife, and her lady-in-waiting live in a brightly painted palace. Their clothes are made from thin linen fabric to keep them cool. The Pharaoh and his wife wear tall, bright headdresses, and everyone is wearing thick, black eyeliner around their eyes.

Tiy (lady-in-waiting)

Ancient Rome

This town square is where all the important business takes place. A Roman citizen wraps himself in a long piece of wool, called a toga, while his wife wears a simple, flowing dress. An army general struts around wearing bright red clothes and a crown of golden leaves.

Felix (Roman citizen)

Ancient China

In a peaceful water garden, an Emperor, an Empress and her court lady admire the views. All three are dressed in flowing robes and dresses made of the finest silks. The ladies wear lots of bright eyeshadow and lipstick, and tie their long hair up on top of their heads.

Emperor Yang

Morgan (lady-in waiting)

Spain in the 1500s

In a Spanish house beside the sea, a count and countess are entertaining a lady visitor. Both women are wearing stiff underskirts called farthingales that make their dresses stand out. The count is wearing a snug jacket called a doublet with a sleeveless over-jacket on top, known as a jerkin. The sleeves of his doublet are decorated with fancy gold patterns and his hat has an ostrich feather on top of it.

Lady Teresa

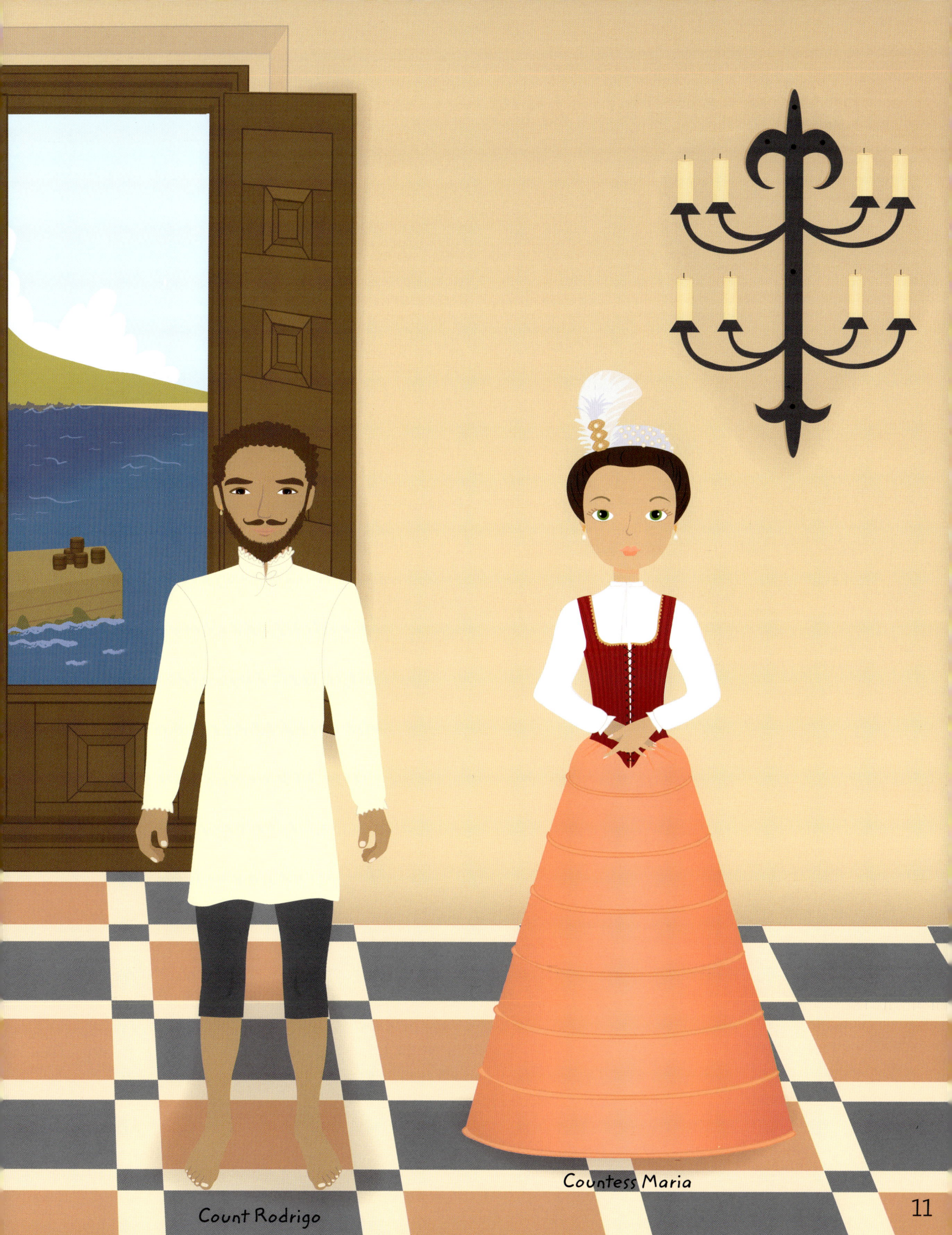

France in the 1770s

A fine lady is strolling in the palace gardens. She wears an elaborate wig with feathers in it. Her skirt is very wide, and her bodice is decorated with layers of lace.

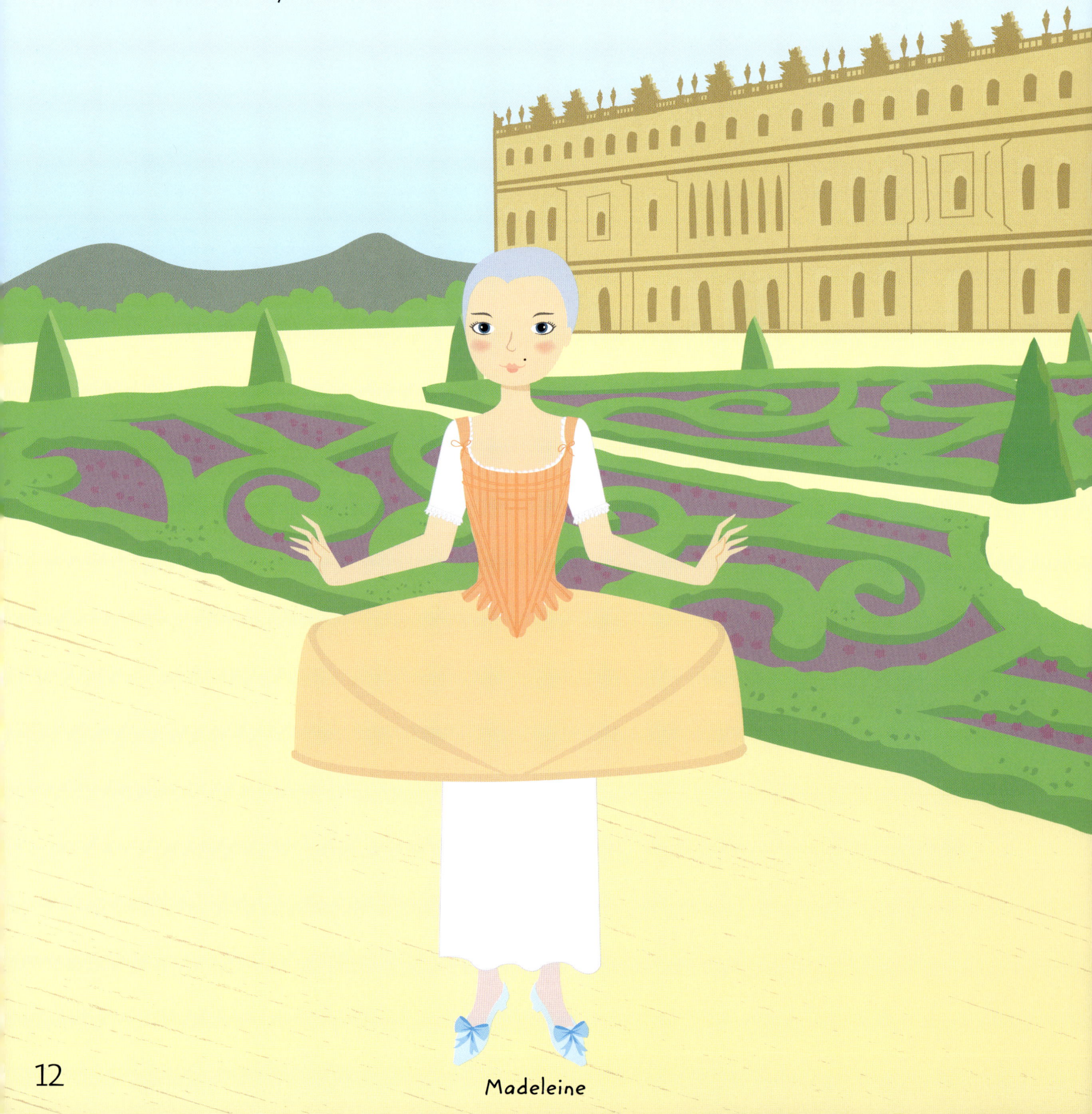

Madeleine

This gentleman is wearing a frilly shirt, a flowery waistcoat, a bright coat and high-heeled shoes with big gold buckles.

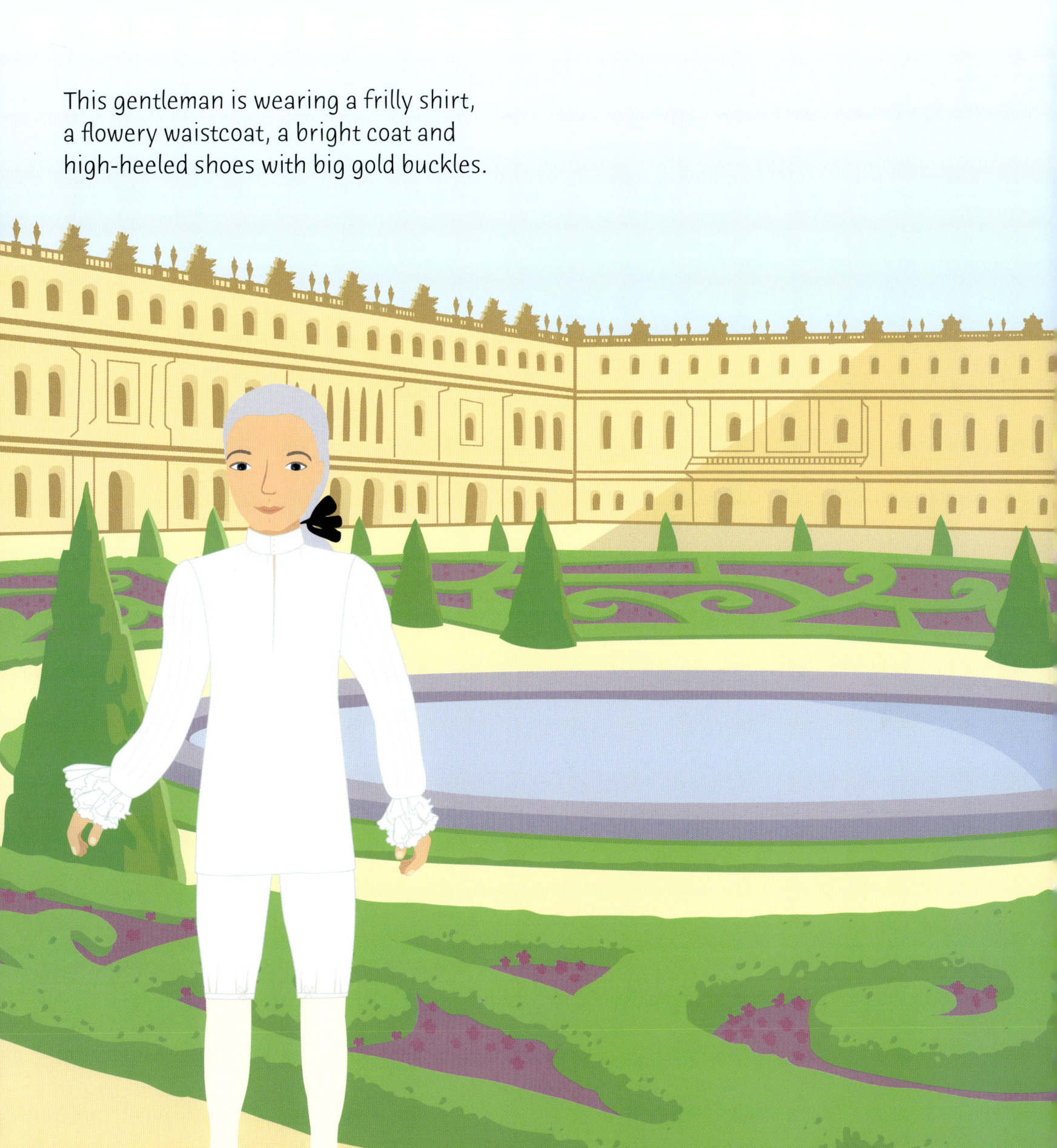

Danton

England (1810)

A handsome officer is visiting a country house, dressed in his bright red uniform. The young lady of the house and her companion are very excited about being visited by such a dashing soldier. The girls are wearing their prettiest summer dresses and are getting ready to go for a walk with him. They put on fancy bonnets and slip delicate silk purses around their wrists.

Lady Charlotte

Edward (officer)

Harriet (Charlotte's companion)

Victorian times (1890s)

These Victorians have put on their finest clothes because they are going to see an opera. The ladies wear tight corsets under their dresses to pull in their waists. The gentleman wears a jacket called a tailcoat and a top hat. When he goes outside, he puts on shoe covers known as spats.

Dorothea

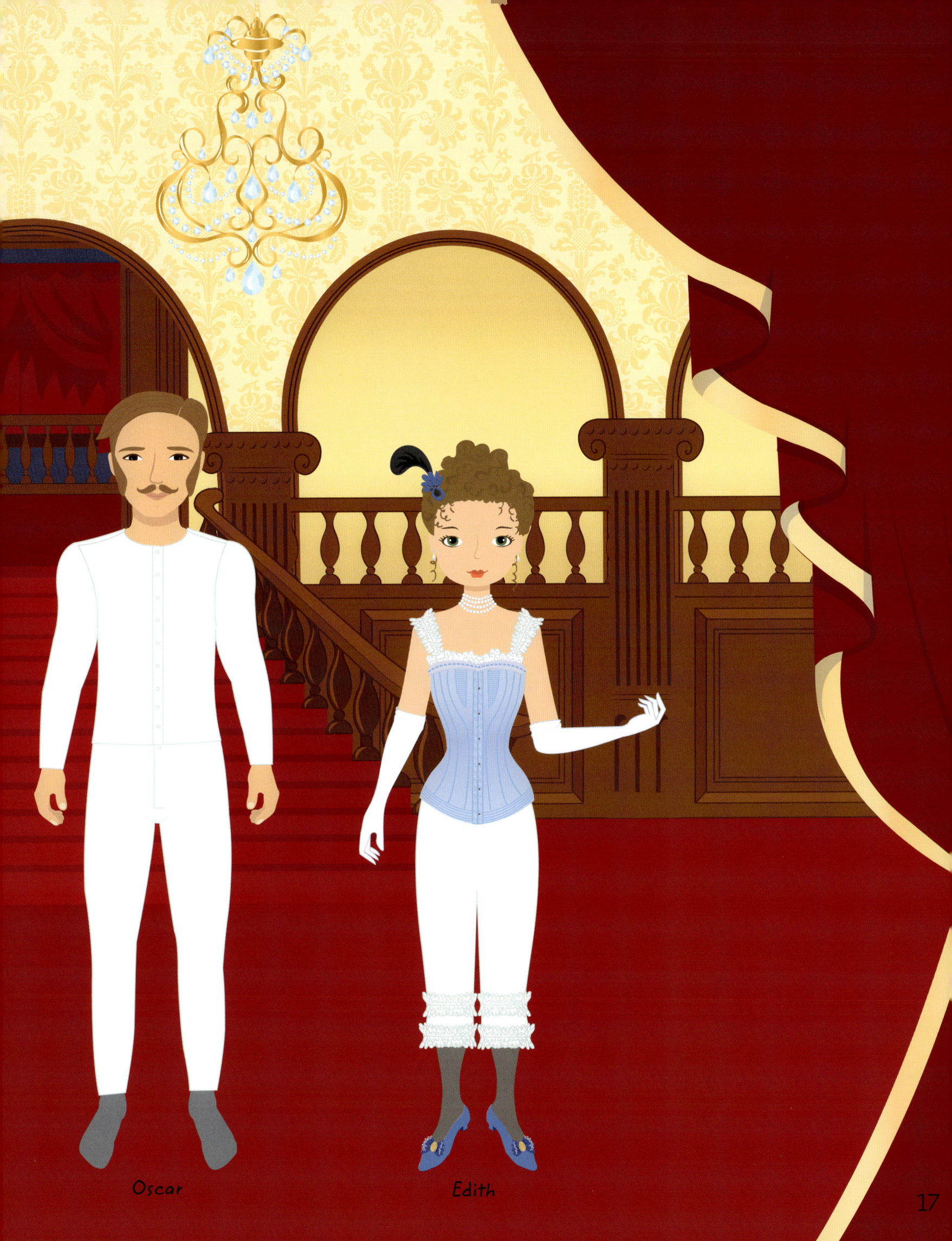

England in the 1920s

It's time for tea and croquet on the lawn of a grand country house. The ladies are wearing knee-length skirts, which have become very fashionable, and their hair is cut short in a 'bob' style. Their gentleman friend is wearing a suit made from a tough type of wool called tweed and his shoes are two different shades.

Cecily

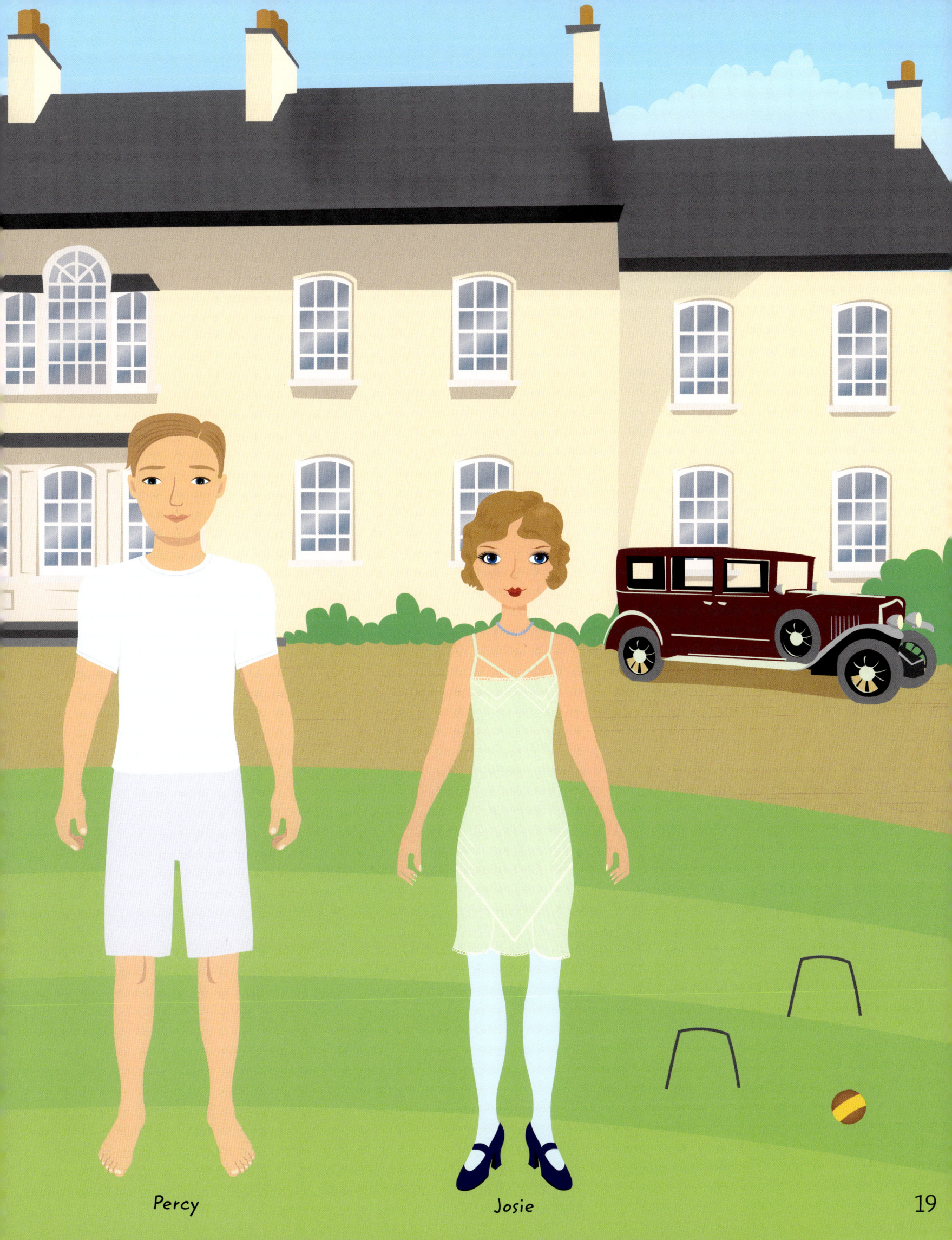

America in the 1950s

These teenagers are hanging out at the local diner, listening to the latest records playing on a juke box. The girls are wearing flat shoes and full skirts that swish when they turn. The boy's bright jacket shows he plays for his college football team.

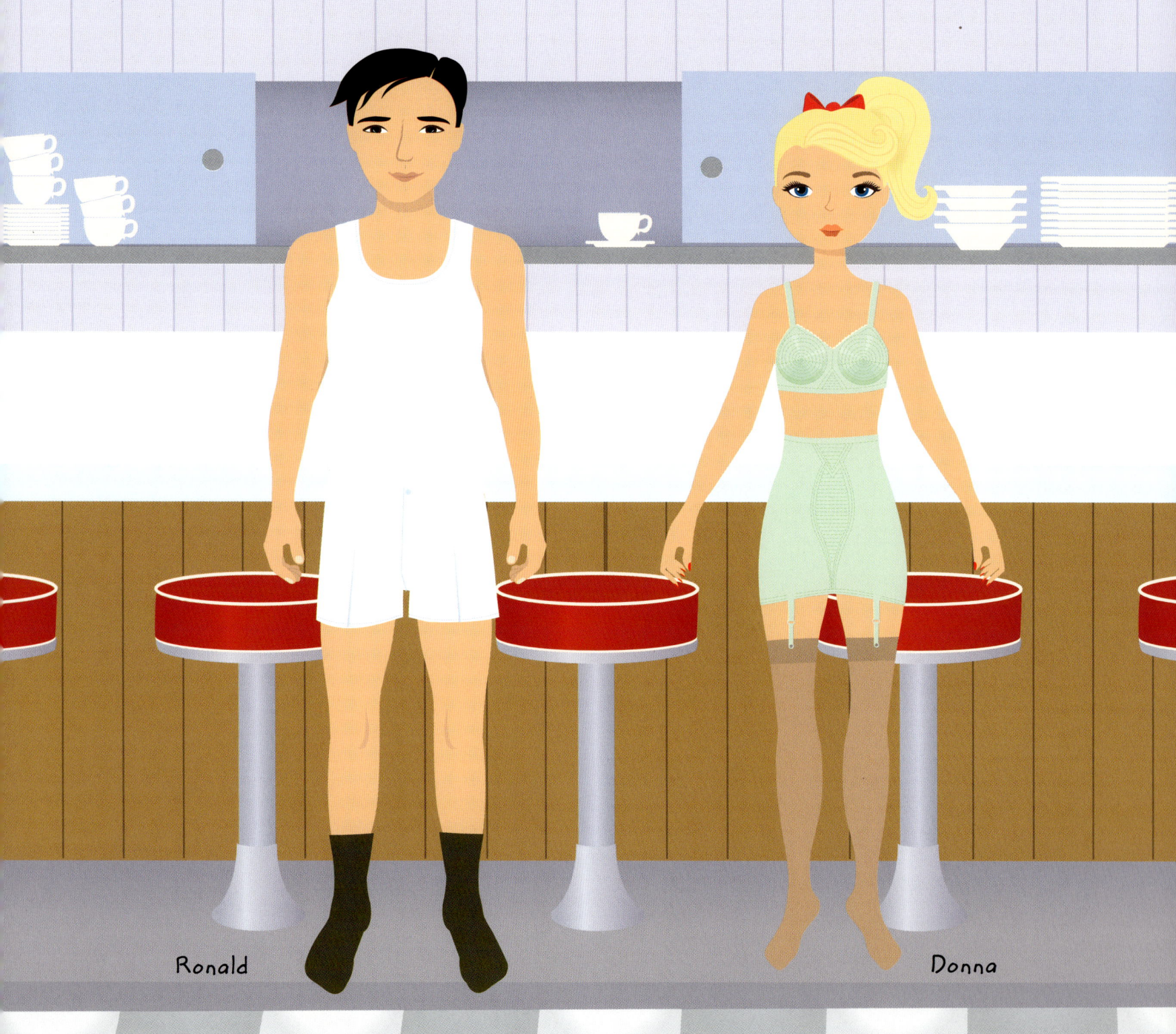

Ronald

Donna

Nancy

London in the 1960s

At an art show, the girls are wearing bold shades and patterns. Their skirts are very short and they wear thick false eyelashes that make their eyes look huge. The man is dressed in a tight-fitting suit, narrow tie and black ankle boots.

Frank

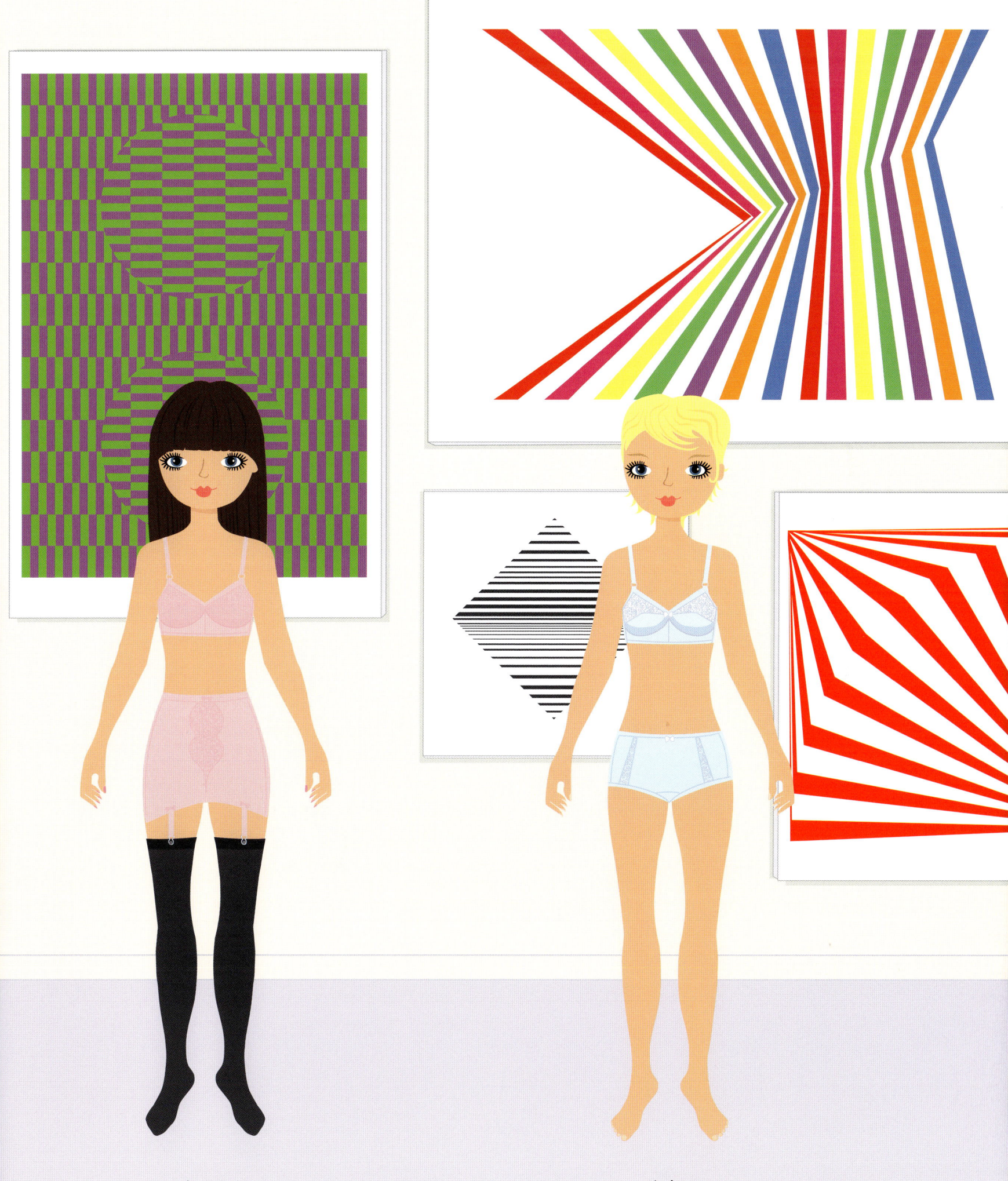

Jean　　　　　　　　　　　　　　　　Helen

Design your own

Now it's your turn. Use some felt-tip pens on the plain stickers to design clothes for these people. What do you think they should wear?